How Abraham Lincoln Used Stories to Touch Hearts, Minds, and Funny Bones

By Terry Sprouse

Doug!   12-15-15

Follow Lincoln's example.

Terry Sprouse

Planeta Books LLC
Tucson, Arizona

ISBN 978-0-9798566-6-2

This publication is designed to provide accurate and authoritative information in regard to the subject matter covered. It is provided with the understanding that neither the author nor the publisher is engaged in rendering legal, accounting or other professional services. If legal or other expert assistance is required, the services of a competent professional person should be sought.

Published by:
Planeta Books LLC
PO Box 41223
Tucson, AZ 85717

For updates and more resources visit:

www.TerrySprouse.com

Acknowledgements

Thank you Randy Cramer, Randy Casarez, Arthur Lohman and Robert Merideth for sharing your editorial expertise with me. Thanks to Phillip Schultz, Randy Lindsey, and Marcia Roberts for providing materials that were very helpful in putting this work together.

I am grateful for Santiago Samorano's outstanding help with the book cover.

Many thanks to the members of *Aztec Toastmasters* who provided discerning feedback on my many "Lincoln Storytelling" speeches. Considerable content from those speeches found its way into the pages of this book.

I acknowledge the immeasurable and unfaltering assistance of my inspiring wife, Angélica (despite her unsubstantiated claims that she taught me everything I know).

Strange that Ulysses does a thousand things so well.

— Iliad

Contents

Introduction

I am not simply a story-teller; it is not the story itself, but its purpose that interests me. -- Abraham Lincoln

The life of Abraham Lincoln is the most intriguing story in American history. Poor farm boy rises, like Venus from the half-shell, against all odds, to become President of the United States. And beyond the Presidency, he achieves legendary status through unparalleled displays of grace, charm, and good humor.

The question in my mind is, "what was the skill that elevated Lincoln to achieve such great heights from such humble beginnings?"

Like all great men and women, he was a mixture of talents and motivations. Lincoln was ambitious, he had a kind disposition, he was a political chess master, and a fine orator. Yet, I believe the one quality of Lincoln, above all else, that allowed him to achieve stratospheric heights, was his humble ability to tell stories.

Stories are the key

Lincoln relentlessly told stories. Not just on special occasions or when the mood was right. He told stories at all times and to everyone. Anytime we read accounts of people who crossed paths with Lincoln, one of the first things they mention is that he told them stories.

Lincoln understood the power of stories. It was a tool that allowed him to quickly and dramatically connect with people, a tool that is available to us as well. We need only follow Lincoln's example.

A legion of books have been written analyzing both

Lincoln's character and his humor. There are more "wit and wisdom of Lincoln" books than you could shake a stovepipe hat at.

But it's not enough just to read or tell the stories of Lincoln, as great as they are. Like an onion, we must peel off the outer layers of Lincoln to find his best kept secrets about: 1) how he developed his skills, 2) the unique personality traits that gave power to his stories, and 3) the techniques he used to present a story.

Emulate Lincoln

One technique that Lincoln used in presenting stories that we can adopt was his personification of the story. Springfield attorney (and student in the law offices of John T. Stuart & Lincoln in 1838) Milton Hay said,

> The secret of Lincoln's success in storytelling was in the active - personified telling of them. Lincoln always enhanced his stories by acting the roles and parts of them with facial expressions, gestures, and movements.

A second Lincoln storytelling technique we can embrace is the inclusion of an inspirational and edifying moral in a story. Secretary of the United States Treasury, Hugh McCullough said,

> Mr. Lincoln's stories were as apt and instructive as the best of Aesop's Fables.

If we would be a true teller of stories we would do well to emulate the Jedi Master of storytelling, and 16th President of the United States, himself.

The goal of this book is to equip you with the very tools that Lincoln used to tell stories. In that vein, I analyze the individual techniques Lincoln used to tell a story and present examples of Lincoln using the same technique. In addition, I describe how Lincoln developed his story telling skills at a young age and the characteristics he possessed that imbued his stories with raw power.

Following Lincoln's lead, I illustrate how I use stories in my daily life and how to "Lincolnize" old stories. In two chapters near the end of the book, I present my absolute favorite stories told by, and told about, Lincoln.

1

The Irresistible Power of Lincoln

Lincoln's story-telling propensity, and the striking fitness of his yarns, was really one of the secrets of his popularity and strength.

-- William Herndon, Lincoln's law partner

How storytelling turbocharged Lincoln's career

Lincoln's remarkable ability to tell stories not only helped open doors for him early in life, but also tipped the scales of history in his favor time-after-time throughout his career.

Lincoln was born September 12, 1808 in Hodgenville, Kentucky. At age 7, young Abe, his father Thomas, mother Nancy, and sister Sarah, moved to Pigeon Creek, Indiana. After Nancy Hanks Lincoln died in 1818, Thomas Lincoln married Sarah Bush in 1819, and in 1830 the Lincoln family moved to a farm near Decatur, Illinois.

When Lincoln moved from his family's farm to the town of New Salem he was 22 years old. Chronicler Edward J. Kempf wrote,

> [Lincoln was] a long, lean, lanky, easy-going, smiling, awkward young stranger, wearing tight, home-made pants shrunken far above his shoe tops.

Despite his peculiar appearance, Lincoln quickly fit into New Salem life. He landed a job in a general store and made friends by telling stories to the customers. As resident Caleb Carman recalled,

> He was liked by every person who knew him. He made himself useful in every way that he could. If the water-bucket was empty he filled it; if wood was needed he chopped it; he was always cheerful and in a good humor.

In 1832, Lincoln volunteered to serve with the Illinois Militia in the Black Hawk War. He was elected captain by the men of his company, most of whom were also from New

Salem. The men knew Lincoln's stories and his kindly demeanor from the general store.

A turning point in Lincoln's life

Following the war, Lincoln ran for a seat in the Illinois State House, and lost. But like a *Timex* watch, "he took a lickin' but kept on tickin'." This political defeat was a turning point in Lincoln's life. Although he lost the election, he won 205 out of 208 votes in his hometown of New Salem. Lincoln realized that the people who knew him best, those who had experienced his good nature and had listened to his stories, they were the people who unanimously voted for him.

Undeterred, he ran for the same office again two years later, but used a new strategy. His approach was to issue no platform statement, make no promises, and give few speeches. Instead, the success or failure of his campaign rested on his own personality alone. He shook hands, told stories, and visited nearly every family in the county. He unleashed the power of his one-on-one storytelling and it won the hearts and votes of his constituents.

In 1836, Lincoln became a lawyer. He again utilized the power of his stories to torpedo opposing lawyers by day and entertain the local populace at night. He continued to connect with people on the campaign trail, and he was elected to the State House for four consecutive terms (1834, 1836, 1838, and 1840).

Stories played a central role in Lincoln's legal career. John Littlefield, a law clerk in the Lincoln-Herndon law office observed,

When he (Lincoln) was introduced to persons, his general method was to entertain them by telling them a story.

Lincoln's motivation

"His ambition was a little engine that knew no rest," wrote William Herndon of his law partner.

Lincoln's ambition emerged at an early age. At 16, Lincoln inscribed this poem into the school notebook of childhood friend Joseph Richardson:

Good boys who to their books apply
Will make great men by & by.

Lincoln's Presidential aide John Hay wrote,

It is absurd to call him a modest man. No great man was ever modest. It was his intellectual arrogance and unconscious assumption of superiority that men like Treasury Secretary Salmon Chase and Senator Charles Sumner never could forgive.

Lincoln told sculptor Henry Volk,

I don't like to hear cut-and-dried sermons. No, when I hear a man preach, I like to see him act as if he were fighting bees!

The same could have been used to describe Lincoln himself when it came to his relentless pursuit of political success. Even if nothing in his outward appearance revealed it, Lincoln's mind was always working at warp speed as if *he* were fighting bees. Lincoln saw every person he met as a potential ally to help him realize his abiding political ambitions. His stories and humor were the first step to draw them into his orbit.

Chicago journalist Horace White said,

[Through storytelling] Mr. Lincoln quickly gained the confidence of strangers, and their affection as well.

If the presidency was the tree that Lincoln aspired to chop down, then storytelling was the ax he would use to do it.

Incubation period - Riding the circuit

Lincoln spent much of his time as a lawyer riding the law circuit in rural Illinois. In the days of the late 1840's and early 1850's, lawyers and judges would travel the "circuit" from small town to small town trying local cases. These small towns were unable to support full-time legal officials, so the circuit riders were the ones to fill the gap.

Lincoln developed and refined his keen storytelling skills while he traveled and worked the circuit. As a trial lawyer, Lincoln crafted stories using language and illustrations that the people could easily grasp. The steady band of new clients, the taking on of new cases, making his circuit in new towns, all presented unique opportunities for Lincoln to accumulate a great repertoire of stories.

Carl Schurz, a Union General who first met Lincoln while riding on a train, commented on Lincoln's uncanny ability to attract followers, in stating,

> I soon felt as if I had known him all my life and we had very long been close friends. He interspersed our conversation with all sorts of quaint stories, each of which had a witty point applicable to the subject at hand.

The epitome of a Lincoln story

This observation by Schurz describes the epitome of a Lincoln story. Lincoln did three things in this example:

1) He connected with the listener. He immediately created a connection between himself and a stranger, so much so that Schurz felt that he and Lincoln had been lifelong friends;

2) He entertained the listener. He made Schurz laugh.

3) He enlightened the listener. He edified Schurz with a relevant point, some food for thought, and conveyed a message Schurz would not soon forget.

Pow! Lincoln knocks the ball out of the park.

Lincoln's Lessons

1) Use storytelling as means to achieve your passion in life. If we set high goals for ourselves we need this powerful tool to make those goals a reality.

2) Telling stories - particularly on a one-to-one personal basis - is a potent technique to connect with people. It is like knowing the secret code to disarm a person's personal alarm system such that you can just walk in the front door and have direct access to their heart.

3) Tell your stories as you "ride your circuit" - in other words, everywhere you go.

4) Practice telling your stories like Lincoln did, to affect people. In other words: Connect. Generate Laughter. Enlighten.

2

They Will Never Forget the Way You Make Them Feel

Those who tell the stories rule the world. -- Plato

Stories are perhaps the most powerful means to communicate ideas. Attaching an idea or an argument to a story increases the probability that a message will be remembered. If you can touch the feelings of a person, you extend the time that a story lives in a person's memory. People may forget the words you say. They may forget who you are, but they will never forget the way you make them feel.

There are two prominent reasons Lincoln told his stories: 1) stories are non-provocative tools of persuasion, and 2) stories are an entertaining and compelling way to connect with people. In addition, Lincoln used stories to fight his own depression, relieve stress, and avoid commitments. His stories disguised the fact when he was telling someone "no." His stories were tools to identify and point out to others flaws in their logic.

Stories are non-provocative tools of persuasion

Lincoln said,

[A story is like] a drop of honey that catches one's heart, which ... when once gained, you will find but little trouble in convincing their judgment of the justice of your cause.

Most people are more receptive to information presented as a story than when presented with a dry, unadorned, and bland fact. Human beings like to think in terms of stories, not in stacks of data. A good story can sweeten a bitter pill. Lincoln didn't force his messages on his people; he let his stories unfold in their own imaginations.

Stories are an entertaining and compelling way to connect with people

Lincoln also said,

Stories are the shortest path between strangers and friends.

Lincoln's version of a *Facebook* page was his one-on-one and face-to-face telling of stories to everyone he met. Stories allowed him to connect with people and win their respect in the shortest possible time. Not a bad skill for a politician to have.

Everyone who walked into Lincoln's law office was told a story before they left. John H. Littlefield observed,

No matter how busy Lincoln might be, whenever anyone came in he would inevitably greet him with a pleasant or funny comment, and before he left would always tell a joke or anecdote. Often he told the same story four or five times in the course of a day (to different visitors), and every time laughed as heartily as anyone.

The many purposes of Lincoln's stories

Lincoln scholar Keith W. Jennison noted,

During the wilderness years he told jokes and stories without trying to prove anything at all; he told them simply because it was natural for him to do so. After he became a lawyer he found that his wit and his acute sense of the ridiculous were effective courtroom tools.

As a politician he handled the weapon of satire as a stiletto or a broad ax as the occasion demanded.

Following are five additional examples of why Lincoln told stories.

1) To replace depression with an anecdote

Lawyers and friends of Lincoln commented that Lincoln would emerge from a seemingly deep depression by telling a funny story.

Judge David Davis (of the *Eighth Circuit Court* in Illinois, the Court where Lincoln practiced law), said that after long days in court,

> If Lincoln was oppressed, the feeling was soon relieved by the narration of a story. The tavern loungers enjoyed it, and his melancholy, taking to itself wings, seemed to fly away.

2) As safety-valve to relieve stress

Do you think that your life is stressful because you have a raving boss and a dysfunctional family life, while at the same time trying to find enough money to make ends meet?

Consider for a moment how stressful Lincoln's life was. He was President during an unpopular war that he seemed to be losing; the majority of his Cabinet members thought that he was an ignoramus and they all could do a better job as President; and, a hysterical wife made his home life seem like *A Nightmare on Elm Street*. If Lincoln had been under any more pressure he would have turned into a diamond.

Given the situation that he found himself, it's only natural that he needed some way to blow off steam and relieve the pressure. He did that though storytelling.

It was common for Lincoln to liven up a Cabinet meeting by telling a story or by reading some humorous quotes from his favorite authors Artemus Ward and Robert Newell (both genial newspaper critics who supported Lincoln's policies.) When nit-picky Cabinet members failed to appreciate the humor as he did, Lincoln reproached them by saying,

> Gentlemen, why don't you laugh? With the fearful strain that is upon me night and day, if I did not laugh occasionally I should die, and you need this medicine as much as I do.

3) To avoid making a commitment

It seemed that nearly everyone (in addition to the aforementioned salted mixed-nuts in the President's Cabinet) thought they could run the county better than Lincoln, and they were not shy about coming to the White House to tell him so.

Lincoln often used stories as a sort of insect repellant against the army ant horde of know-it-alls who came to his office with their harebrained schemes. Herndon observed Lincoln's methods as,

> . . . Swinging around what he suspected was the vital point, but never nearing it, interlacing his answers with a seemingly endless supply of stories and jokes.

Visitors would leave his office feeling they had persuaded the president to their way of thinking, but once having walked only a few blocks they realized they had been bamboozled by Lincoln's tricky verbal manipulations, or as Herndon put it,

> [After] blowing away the froth of Lincoln's humorous narratives, they would find nothing left.

4) To soften the blow of having to tell someone "no"

Lincoln received many "favor seekers" to his office. Often they were upset because he had fired a relative who was in line to become a general, or because he backed a program that ran against their interest, or he failed to give a job to a "qualified" candidate. Lincoln politely welcomed them all and immediately waylaid them with a story. These visitors left his company without what they came for but with only with what they were given: a story with a message for them to think about.

One example of how Lincoln used stories to soften a refusal was when Senator John Creswell (a loyal Republican supporter of Lincoln) came to Lincoln to request the release of an old friend who had been captured and imprisoned.

Creswell admitted,

> I know the man has acted like a fool, but he is my friend, and a good fellow; let him out; give him to me, and I will be responsible that he will have nothing further to do with the rebels.

Lincoln contemplated the request. It reminded him of a group of young people who went on a little country excursion. They crossed a shallow stream in a flatboat, but on their way back they found that the boat had disappeared. So each boy picked up a girl and carried her across, until the only ones remaining were a little short chap and a great "Gothic-built" old maid. Lincoln complained,

> Now Creswell, you are trying to leave me in the same predicament. You fellows are all getting your friends out of this scrape; and you will succeed in carrying off one after another, until nobody but Jeff Davis [President of the Confederate States] and myself will be left, and then I won't know what to do. How should I feel? How should I look, lugging him over?

5. To point out flaws in logic

Combined with his rapier wit, Lincoln's proclivity for logic enabled him to point out the absurdity of an argument with a casual jest.

Supporters of an applicant for the position of Commissioner of the Hawaiian Islands tried to convince Lincoln that their man was both competent for the post but also in dire need it because the climate was good his health.

Lincoln responded:

> Gentlemen, there are eight other applicants for that position, and they are all sicker'n your man.

Lincoln's Lessons

1) If we wish to persuade someone we must wrap our idea in a story.

2) Tell stories just for the fun of it.

3) Tell stories as a tool in your profession.

4) Tell stories to replace depression, relieve stress, avoid commitments, soften a blow, or to point out flaws in logic.

3

Young Abe Extends Storytelling to Unexplored Regions

Towering genius disdains a beaten path. It seeks regions hitherto unexplored. -- Abraham Lincoln

As a boy growing up in rural Illinois, Lincoln soaked up the fundamentals of wisdom and the secrets of life. He was guided, like a ship drawn to a lighthouse, by several strong influences in his young life. These included his father's storytelling skills, his step-mother's encouragement, the books that fortuitously fell into his hands, and the many opportunities he had to practice his skills. Some of these experiences he accepted at face value, but others he would reformulate, and test by fire, for a higher purpose.

The fruit does not fall far from the tree

Thomas Lincoln may not have been the best father, but he had a quick wit, a gift for mimicry, and great memory for funny stories. These qualities Thomas passed down to his son. They became the greatest gifts Lincoln ever received. Young Abe listened so intently to his father's stories, words molded from the clay of everyday experiences, that they were burned onto the hard drive of his memory.

Lincoln recalled after listening to adults talk in the evening, that he spent,

> no small part of the night walking up and down, and trying to make out what was the exact meaning of some of their, to me, dark sayings.

Instead of sleeping, he would turn the conversations over in his mind until, as he recalled,

> I had put it in language plain enough, as I thought, for any boy I knew to comprehend.

The next day, Lincoln would stand on a tree trunk and

regale his young friends with the stories he had heard the night before. He appreciated the warm response mixed with laughter his stories evoked from his friends. The storytelling skills he was assimilating would one day serve him well as both a lawyer and a politician, but not before other pieces of the puzzle were in place.

(Step) Mother knows best

When Sarah Bush became Thomas Lincoln's second wife and Abe's stepmother, she brought along with her three children and all her worldly possessions, including such books as *Aesop's Fables, Robinson Crusoe,* and *Pilgrim's Progress.* These books were to Abe Lincoln what receiving a first *iPad* would be to a child today. It was an imagination-bending porthole to a whole new world. The information that Lincoln assimilated from these books, especially *Aesop's Fables,* became the raw material for later storytelling.

Books became the "college education" that Lincoln never received formally. They united his mind with the great minds of the past. Like the fusion of two atomic particles, the coming together of Lincoln and the wisdom initially provided by Sarah Bush Lincoln's books, would ignite Lincoln's vast, dormant potential.

With his stepmother's love and guidance, Lincoln made rapid progress. "He read all the books he could get his hands on," she recalled, and was already practicing writing and speaking at an early age. Lincoln would listen to a Sunday sermon at church then reenact it for the other children, and "almost repeat it word for word." She remembered,

He must understand everything even to the smallest thing - minutely and exactly, he would then repeat it over to himself again and again - some times in one form and then in another and when it was fixed in his mind he . . . never lost that fact or his understanding of it.

Fables are everywhere

Carl Sandburg points out the one book that made a lasting impression on young Lincoln was *Aesop's Fables*. Sandburg says,

> As he read through the book a second and third time, he had a feeling there were fables all around, that everything he saw and heard had a fable wrapped around it somewhere.

Lincoln was moved by the wisdom and beauty of proverbs such as, "Muzzle not the ox that treads out the corn" and "He that rules his own spirit is greater than he that takes a city."

In reading through the fables, Lincoln realized that animals, plows, hammers, fingers, toes, people, and all things had fables connected with them. There is an outside appearance to things, which most people observed, but the real message remained hidden inside, like the peanut inside a shell.

Fables and morals became a part of Lincoln's stories. His stories did more than just entertain people. With this piece of the puzzle discovered and put into place, Lincoln's stories were tinged with a new power.

Storytelling in the school of hard knocks

Lincoln learned to be a good storyteller through trial and error. His school was the school of hard knocks. He didn't have a professional speech coach, or high school debate team, or instructional movies in his curriculum. Lincoln's classroom was wherever he happened be telling a story.

His exam results were etched in the faces of the audience who listened to his stories. If the story worked, he was rewarded with a positive response. If the story didn't work, he tweaked it the next time to make it better. The only way to improve was to tell more stories to others, and be graded by more audiences. Like proposing matrimony, it may be scary, but there is only one way to do it.

Lincoln puts the pieces together

Lincoln took the raw material laid before him and formed the most powerful tool in the world. He used what his father taught him about storytelling and extended it to unexplored regions. Storytelling became a magic wand waved to win over thousands of friends and followers.

Many people know of "Aesop's Fables" and other great books. Yet, Lincoln not only read them, he let them flow though his soul and transform his deepest concepts of life. Countless individuals have experienced the school of hard knocks. Lincoln paid his dues to the extent that he created his own private universe. A place where, as Herndon noted, the truth expressed in stories is revered as highly as the truth found in the scientific disciplines of math, chemistry, and physics. With all the puzzle pieces together, Lincoln became a mighty force of nature, the likes of which had not been seen before or since.

Profound, yet fundamental, principles were in play. Some people only scratch the surface of life and do the simply apparent, superficial tasks and pursue shallow success. Others have the ability to penetrate the surface. Through pure doggedness and grit they claw out the underlying truth, perceive how dissimilar parts fit together, and then cling to their revelations with a death grip.

Lincoln's Lessons

1) Learn to listen to the stories of others with the intention of later repeating what you heard.

2) Learn to reformulate stories to ensure that: a) you clearly understand the story's message and; b) other people, through your skill, grasp it as well.

3) Look beyond the surface and immediate appearance of things; discover the fables that reside within.

4) Assimilate audience feedback into your stories.

5) Never miss an opportunity to tell a story.

6) Piece together wisdom you unearth in new and original ways.

7) Be faithful to your vision.

4

Give Each Character a Personality

His stories may be literally retold, every word, period and comma, but the real humor perished with Lincoln; he provoked as much laughter by the grotesque expression of his homely face as by the abstract fun of his stories.

-- Henry C. Whitney, Lawyer

Lincoln used body language, facial expressions, and voice mimicking to make a story effective. His techniques become clear when we look at an example. One of Lincoln's favorite stories describes an unfortunate encounter between a lizard and a country preacher.

"The Little Blue Lizard"

A preacher back in Indiana was delivering a sermon in a log meeting house in the woods. The preacher was wearing old fashioned baggy pantaloons fastened with one button and no suspenders. His shirt was fastened at the neck with one button. In a loud voice the preacher announced his text for the day. "I am the Christ whom I shall represent this day." About that time a little blue lizard ran up one leg of the pantaloons. The preacher went ahead with his sermon, slapping at his legs. After a while the lizard came so high the preacher got desperate, and, going on with his sermon, unbuttoned his pants, let them fall down and kicked them off.

By this time the lizard had changed his route and was circling around under his shirt. The preacher repeating his text, "I am the Christ whom I shall represent today." Loosened his shirt button and off came the shirt. The congregation sat in the pews dazed and dazzled. Everything was still for a minute, then a dignified old lady stood, pointed a finger at the pulpit and called out at the top of her voice: "I just want to say, sir, that if you represent Jesus Christ, then I'm done with the Bible."

"Be the ball, Danny"

In the movie *Caddyshack*, Chevy Chase famously instructed his young golf protégé,

> Danny, there's a force in the universe that makes things happen. And all you have to do is get in touch with it, stop thinking, let things happen, and be the ball.

Likewise, one of Lincoln's storytelling secrets was his ability "to be the story," or, by putting himself so much into the story and into each character of the story, he and the story became one.

William Herndon said,

> Lincoln's power of mimicry and his manner of recital were unique. His countenance and all his features seemed to take part in the performance.

Do's and don'ts of Lincoln storytelling

Here are the "do's" and "don'ts" in the Lincoln school of storytelling:

Do:

- Give each character a personality: a voice, a stance, a way of moving.
- Use words to vocalize an emotion, and use facial expressions to visualize the emotion.
- Add interest to your voice by varying your rate of delivery, your volume, your pitch, your inflections, and your word emphasis.

Don't:

- Be overly melodramatic; keep expressions and gestures subtle.
- Be afraid to have some fun.

For a great example of using body language and facial expressions to communicate, watch Charlie Chaplin in the boxing scene from his masterpiece "City Lights" (search "Charlie Chaplin boxing" on *YouTube*). In this classic "fish out of water" scene, Chaplain's ill-prepared character displays all the idiosyncrasies of a boxer down to the smallest details. By making the situation as real as possible to us, the humor becomes all the more hilarious. That's the type of imitation that we strive for when we tell our stories.

Learn to mimic voices

Much of Lincoln's success as a story teller was due to a talent for mimicry. Author T. G. Onstot said,

> In the role of story-teller, I never knew his equal. His power of mimicry was very great. He could perfectly mimic any accent.

In my case, I have several standard voices in my repertoire. I use voices of famous actors as voices for the characters in my stories. Some of the voices I use are John Wayne (for any cowboy-type, or tough-guy character), Jimmy Stewart (for a father figure), Henry Fonda (for Lincoln, or "good guy" characters), Jack Nicholson (for bad or slimy guys), a teenager whose voice is breaking (for teenagers or scattered brained characters), *Eeyore*, from *Winnie the Pooh*, or *Goofy*, (for a slow thinker or a frightened person).

Here are some tips on how to mimic voices:

1) Watch videos on *YouTube* of the person you want to imitate;

2) Practice saying the same words that they say;

3) Include catch phrases that the character uses, such as "You can't handle the truth!" for Jack Nicholson and using the word "Pilgrim" for imitating John Wayne;

4) Practice by testing bits of your impression on family and friends until you feel comfortable using it in a story;

5) Practice at least four times a day;

6) Make a video of yourself doing impressions;

7) If you teach, as I sometimes do (as a long-term substitute teacher), practice using different voices for each character when you read a book to the class. For example, when I read a *Winnie the Pooh* story to a class, I use my teenager voice for *Winnie the Pooh*, a high pitched voice for *Piglet*, a deep and slow voice for *Eeyore*, a fast paced and enthusiastic voice for *Tigger*;

8) If you have children or grandchildren, or nieces and nephews, it's another great opportunity to read stories and practice voices for different characters.

In developing a "minister voice" for the "Blue Lizard" story, and for the "Teeth Will Be Provided" story (see below),

I watched videos of Reverend Lovejoy from *The Simpsons*, Jim Carry as *Reverend Carl Pathos*, and some old black-and-white videos of travelling evangelist preachers, such as A. A. Allen. Some keys to learning the minister voice were to speak slowly, to deepen my voice at the end of a sentence, to stretch out the last word of each sentence, and to incorporate a slight southern twang.

Don't worry if your impersonations are not perfect. Mine never are. Impersonations just need to be good enough to allow the audience to identify the characters.

Performing the "Little Blue Lizard" story

Now let's take another look at the "Little Blue Lizard" story. This time let's examine the way that Lincoln told it and analyze the storytelling techniques that Lincoln used. The objective is for you to be able to tell the story like Lincoln did.

This is one of my favorite Lincoln stories to tell because:

1) It's fun to tell, and

2) The audience appreciates the story because of the way Lincoln humorously presented it.

> A preacher back in Indiana was delivering a sermon in a log meeting house in the woods. *Imitate the preacher by standing straight, hands grasp collar of shirt, self-important look on face.*
>
> The preacher was wearing old fashioned baggy pantaloons fastened with one button and no suspenders. His shirt was fastened at the neck with one

button. In a loud voice the preacher announced his text for the day, "I am the Christ whom I shall represent this day." U*se loud preacher voice like Reverend Lovejoy, or any stereotypical southern preacher. Speak slowly, stretch out the words, and have fun with it.*

About that time a little blue lizard ran up one leg of the pantaloons. The preacher went ahead with his sermon, slapping at his legs. G*lace down, slowly slap your and lower leg and work your way up the leg slapping a little faster as you go, maintain eye contact with the audience, put a perplexed look on your face.*

After a while the lizard came so high the preacher got desperate, and, going on with his sermon, unbuttoned his pants, let them fall down and kicked them off. *Pantomime loosening the waistband button and kicking off the pants with one foot.*

By this time the lizard had changed his route and was circling around under his shirt. S*lap your hands around your shirt as if trying to hit the moving target.*

The preacher repeating his text, "I am the Christ whom I shall represent today" (*preacher voice*) loosened his shirt button and off came the shirt. P*antomime loosening the collar button and pulling the shirt off over your head.*

The congregation sat in the pews dazed and dazzled.

Everything was still for a minute, then a dignified old lady stood, pointed a finger at the pulpit and called out at the top of her voice: "I just want to say, sir, that if you represent Jesus Christ, then I'm done with the Bible." *Scrunch up your body like a little old granny, use an angry granny voice like Granny Clampett from the "Beverly Hillbillies," or the Granny from the "Sylvester and Tweety" cartoons, speak slowly, and shake your finger at the preacher.*

Example of Lincoln Mimicry Story

"Teeth Will Be Provided"

The fiery Irish minister was preaching on the End Times - and in particular on the Day of Judgment. As he reached the climax of his address he said that on the Day of Judgment "You will all wail and gnash your teeth."

At which point an old woman raised her hand and said, "Preacher, I ain't got no teeth."

The Minister replied, "Madam, on this great Judgment Day, teeth will be provided. "

Like The "Little Blue Lizard," this Lincoln story uses the same two characters, the preacher and the little old lady. Consequently, the same voices and gestures would apply here.

Lincoln's Lessons

1) Use mimicry, facial expressions, and body language to enhance a story.

2) Practice a new voice four times a day.

3) Don't worry about being perfect when you mimic a voice, just get close enough so the characters are distinguishable.

5

Use Self-deprecating Humor

I leave it to my audience. If I had another face, do you think I would be wearing this one?

-- Abraham Lincoln, during a debate with Stephen Douglas

Lincoln knew that he was not a handsome man. At 6'4" tall and weighing only 175 pounds, one neighbor called him "thin as a beanpole and ugly as a scarecrow." Political opponents referred to him as a "baboon" or an "ugly ape." Not one to take such attacks personally, Lincoln was able to deflect unkind comments and even capitalize on criticism by making himself the butt of many of his own best jokes. He had no illusions about his personal appearance and joked about it so often that he turned his homeliness into an asset.

Look for ways to poke fun at yourself

Look for things about you that stand out: Are you a big person, a short person, a person with an accent? Do you use a wheel chair? Do you wear glasses? Are you bald? Are you a high energy person? Do you speak slowly? Anything that stands out, that is unique or special about you, is a possible target for self-deprecation.

Here are some ways I use self-deprecating humor. I am not super tall and thin like Lincoln, but I do have other outstanding physical characteristics. These include:

1. I am skinny.

2. I wear glasses.

3. I have big ears.

Here are ways that I address these characteristics with self-deprecating humor:

Skinny

"I'm so thin, I have to run around in the shower to get wet."

Wear glasses

"I only wear glasses so that I can do that dramatic removal."

Big ears

"I'm Terry Sprouse. And these are my ears." (per Mark Katz*)*.

Examples of Lincoln's self-deprecating humor

"Stay at Home"

> Speaking at a banquet held by newspaper editors at Decatur, Illinois on February 22, 1856, Lincoln apologized for being present, explaining that not being an editor he felt out of place. He illustrated his feelings by telling of an extremely ugly man who, riding along a narrow road, was met by a woman.
>
> As she passed the woman looked at him intently and finally observed: "Well, you are the ugliest man I ever saw."
>
> "Perhaps so," admitted the unfortunate fellow, somewhat crestfallen, "but I can't help that, madam."
>
> "No, I suppose not," agreed the woman, "but you might stay at home."

"Knife on a Train"

A man approached Lincoln on a train, saying: "Excuse me, sir, but I have an article in my possession which rightfully belongs to you."

"How is that?" asked Lincoln in amazement.

Whereupon the stranger produced a jack-knife and explained: "This knife was placed in my hands some years ago, with the injunction that I was to keep it until I found a man uglier than myself. Allow me now to say, sir, that I think you are fairly entitled to it."

"Prepare to Die"

One day when I first came to Springfield I got into a fit of musing in my room and stood resting my elbows on the bureau. Looking into the glass, it struck me what an ugly man I was. The fact grew on me and I made up my mind that I must be the ugliest man in the world. It so maddened me that I resolved, should I ever see an uglier man, I would shoot him on sight.

Not long after this "Archie" (naming a lawyer present) – came to town and the first time I saw him I said to myself, "There's the man." I went home, took down my gun and prowled the streets waiting for him. He soon came along.

"Halt, Archie," said I, pointing the gun at him, "say your prayers, for I am going to shoot you."

"Why, Mr. Lincoln, what's the matter, what have I done?"

"Well, I made an oath that if I ever saw an uglier man than I, I'd shoot him on the spot. You are uglier, so make ready to die."

"Mr. Lincoln, do you really think I am uglier than you?

"Yes."

"Well, Mr. Lincoln," said Archie deliberately, and looking me squarely in the face, "if I am any uglier, fire away."

Lincoln's Lessons

1) Deflect attacks by appropriating your opponent's criticism of you.

2) Make fun of your own outstanding characteristics.

3) Use self-deprecating humor when you feel out of place. It will endear you to your audience.

6

Add a Moral to the Story

In order to win a man to your cause, you must first reach his heart, the great high road to his reason.

– Abraham Lincoln

Lincoln's stories as a younger man were told for purposes of generating laughter or to win an argument. When Lincoln became President, the focus of his stories shifted to frequently include morals. He used stories to gently show people who disagreed with his policies the logical reasoning behind his decisions.

Alternately, Lincoln could have refused to meet with those who opposed him, but that would have caused their doubts to fester and generated even more hostile feelings. His response was to view their perspectives as being no different than his own, as if he were in their shoes.

He didn't view them as enemies. He viewed them as he did his childhood friends. They just needed things explained in the proper terms for them to fully grasp and support Lincoln's view.

Lincoln's goal was never to knock down his enemies like a row of bowling pins, but rather he aimed to convince them to fall down voluntarily. Stories were the way he reached their hearts and minds.

Lincoln friend and author, Alexander McClure, observed,

> While nearly all of Lincoln's stories have a humorous side, they also contain a moral, which every good story should have. They contain lessons that could be taught so well in no other way. Every one of them is a sermon. Lincoln, like the Man of Galilee, spoke to the people in parables.

Examples of Lincoln's stories that have a moral

"The Hog is on Both Sides of the Creek"

Listening to two groups of men that came to argue as to whether or not a St. Louis church should be closed as a result of statements of disloyalty from its minister, Lincoln said that the situation reminded him of a story. He said that a man in Sangamon County (Illinois) had a melon patch that kept getting ruined by a wild hog. Finally, he and his sons decided to take their guns and track the animal down. They followed the tracks to the neighboring creek, where they disappeared. Then, they discovered tracks on the opposite bank, and waded through. They kept on the trail a couple of hundred yards, when the tracks again went into the creek, and promptly turned up on the other side.

Out of breath and patience, the farmer said "John you cross over and go up on that side of the creek, and I'll keep up on this side, because I believe that hog is on both sides of the creek!"

"Gentlemen," concluded Lincoln, "that is just where I stand in regard to your controversies in St. Louis. I am on both sides. I can't allow my Generals to run the churches, and I can't allow your ministers to preach rebellion."

"The Woodman's Daughter"

During a conversation with W.C. Reeves (a Virginia supporter of Lincoln), just prior to the outbreak of the Civil

War, Reeves advised President Lincoln to appease the South and let them have Fort Sumter and all other government property in the Southern states without a fight.

"Do you remember the fable of the woodman's daughter?" Lincoln asked. Reeves had not.

"A lion," said the President, "was very much in love with a woodman's daughter. The fair maid referred him to her father. The lion applied for the girl."

The father replied, "Your teeth are too long."

The lion went to a dentist and had them extracted. Returning, he asked for the bride.

"No," said the woodman, "your claws are too long."

Going back to the dentist, he had them drawn. Then he returned to claim his bride, and the woodman, seeing that he was unarmed beat out his brains."

Lincoln concluded, "May it not be so with me, if I give up all that is asked to appease the South?"

"Trust Blondin to Cross Niagara Falls"

Some gentlemen from the West had called at the White House and harangued Mr. Lincoln in an excited manner about the omissions and commission of the government. He heard them patiently for a time, and finally said:

Gentlemen, suppose all the property you were worth

was in gold, and you had put it in the hands of *Blondin* (the first tightrope walker to cross *Niagara Falls,* in 1860) to carry across the Niagara Falls on a tight rope. Would you shake the rope while he was passing over it, or keep shouting to him, "Blondin, stoop a little more; go a little faster?"

No, I am sure you would not. You would hold your breath as well as your tongue, and keep your hands off until he was safely over. Now, the government is in the same situation, and is carrying across a stormy ocean an immense weight; untold treasures are in its hands; it is doing the best it can; don't badger it; keep silence, and it will get you safely over.

Lincoln's Lessons

1) Use a moral in your story to gently win over your opponents.

2) Try to view the world as others see it.

3) Explain yourself as clearly as possible, just like you would to your best friend.

7

How I Use Stories in Daily Life

They say I tell a great many stores and I reckon I do, but I believe that common people, are more easily informed through the medium of a broad illustration than in any other way.

– Abraham Lincoln

Not everyone is a born storyteller, myself included. My natural inclination is to leave the spotlight to the extroverts. However, I find if I make a little effort, I can overcome my introvert tendencies and share my experiences with others through personal stories. The amount of effort I make is directly related to how well I am focused in on my aspirations.

I don't wish to be President like Lincoln, but some of the things that drive me to be more outgoing and share stories are my goals, including, to be (1) a proficient public speaker, (2) an articulate guest on radio and television shows, (3) a good father who passes my knowledge along to my children, and (4) a better landlord and good communicator with my tenants.

Our stories don't need to be great. Not all of Lincoln's stories were earth-shattering. Not all your stories need to elicit hilarious laughter or have a strong message, like Lincoln's best stories did. Most stories that I tell are more mundane, but they still accomplish the purpose of connecting with other people.

Stories as a teaching tool

Stories are a useful teaching tool with my two teenage sons. I can no longer use the direct technique with them, and just say, "Stop doing that or you can't play *Xbox*!" That approach is a dead end. It would just result in an argument and hard feelings.

If I really want to mold their behavior, I talk to them when they are relaxed, like in the car. I tell them an interesting story (at least to me) from my past experience that reflects some point that I want to make. Sometimes I wonder if my boys are really paying attention to my "rambling reminisces." But, when they later ask me for more details about a story that

I have told, I realize that maybe my story has struck a chord with them.

"Shake Every Hand in the Room"

This is a story I tell my boys about the power of politeness.

When I was a Peace Corps Volunteer in Honduras I lived in a small town where the only way to make a long distance call home was to go to the phone company. (In prehistoric times before smart phones.)

First, I would have to stand in a long line of people to give my phone number to the two telephone operators. Then, I would sit down in one of the chairs around the side of the room. When the connection was made I would be called up to the front desk to talk to my relatives on one of the only two telephones. Sometimes it could take an hour or two before the call went through. About once a month I called my mother or my Aunt Fran.

After a few episodes of this process I noticed that even though I followed the steps the same as the other patrons, there were those who would get there phone calls put through much sooner than I would. At first I thought that my calls went through slower because I was the only *gringo* in a room full of Hondurans. As I sat there waiting for my call to go through, I observed how one guy in particular, Eduardo, always got his calls put though the fastest. I realized that he was also the most friendly and outgoing guy in the waiting room.

When it was his turn to give his phone number to the receptionists, he engaged them in friendly conversation. He'd say,

"Hi, how are you today?"

"Nice blouse."

"How are the kids?"

Then, he walked around and shook hands with everyone in the room, including me, saying:

"Hi, nice to see you."

After a ridiculously short time, his call was placed well ahead of other people who had preceded him in line.
I soon started using Eduardo's techniques. I chatted up the secretaries, and shook hands with everybody in the room, and my calls suddenly starting going through much faster than before.

The moral is:

"If you don't shake every hand, you can't talk to Aunt Fran."

"Dog's Best Friend"

When one of my boys was playing too rough with our mild-mannered dog Blackie, I said,

When I was your age, I had a little dog named 'Spot.' His body was all white except for one brown spot on his back. One day I took Spot for a walk, and afterwards I was in a hurry to go play with my friends. So instead of opening the gate, I just dropped Spot over the fence into the back yard.

Later that day, I noticed that Spot was limping on one of his back legs.

My Mother said, 'Spot hurt his leg because you dropped him over the fence.'

We took Spot to the veterinarian, and he had to wear a cast on his leg for six weeks. I felt horribly bad about the way I treated Spot.

The same thing can happen with Blackie, if you're too rough with her. You might not intend to hurt her, but she still might get hurt."

I concluded by telling my son that my philosophy about dogs is: "Properly trained, a man can be *dog's* best friend."

Stories created during interviews

Often I use stories when I have radio or TV interviews to promote my books. My goal as a radio guest is to inform the audience and to entertain them. If I am a guest on the radio show, I usually come on near the end of the show. I like to tune into the show an hour or two before I appear, so that I can listen to the host and make up a humorous comment or story that will tie into something he has said earlier in the show.

"Put Millionaire Baseball Players Back to Work"

Not long ago, there were a lot of stories in the news about Alex Rodriguez, the New York Yankees center fielder, who was being suspended for steroid use. I was listening to the radio news reports about Rodriguez before I went on the air. When it was my time to be the guest, I worked this story into the interview about my real estate book.

I said to the host,

Steve, I have been getting some emails from this guy named Alex Rodriguez. Apparently, he is in the process of making a career change, and he wants a free copy of my book. I feel sorry for the poor guy. He's like a lost puppy. In the interest of striking a blow against unemployment, and so he can get a fresh start, I may just send him a copy.

"Don't Get Caught Fishing and Sewing"

A radio host in New Jersey had a segment on his show entitled "Weird New Jersey Laws" just prior to my interview. The law, established around 1889, states that persons attempting to fish and sew at the same time are subject to arrest. One can only imagine the horrible threat to public safety if desperate criminals attempt to evade this law.

Before my segment ended, Dave, the host, asked me, "Do you have any final comments?" I was ready for that question, and had been cooking up an appropriate response. I said,

You know Dave, once I retire from the real estate business, I had considered New Jersey as a nice place to settle down. Then, this morning, I heard your report on the "Fishing and Sewing" Law on the books in New Jersey. Since I like to fish and my wife likes to sew, and we do it at the same time, we could be hauled off to the slammer. So, needless to say, we are reconsidering our choice of places to retire.

Naturally, my response was off topic, and designed to get a rise from Dave. But, it allowed my segment to end on a humorous and memorable note.

Prefabricated stories

I also like to pull out stories from my books to use during radio interviews. Here are a few that I have frequently used.

"Partners in Work and Marriage"

My wife and I are partners in both marriage and in our real estate business. We simply started our business with buying an inexpensive fixer-upper house, one that had been repossessed by a bank. We moved into and lived in the fixer-upper house while we did the necessary repairs. But most important, we did not sell our original home. We rented it out.

Who says married couples can't be business partners? And the great thing is we have never considered divorce . . . murder sometimes, but never divorce.

"Karma vs. Dogma"

After going through my explanation about how everyone can learn to repair a house, a friend of mine insisted that it was impossible for him to do fix-up work; it just wasn't in his genes. I replied that his way of thinking was his dogma. My karma told me that he could do it. In time, little by little, he did learn to make repairs and he came to enjoy it, even relish it.

My karma ran over his dogma.

"Work like Dogs"

Some self-proclaimed "experts" will try to convince you that operating a real estate business is a piece of cake. Don't believe them. If it was easy, everybody would be doing it.

Repairing houses is hard work. Don't expect it to be easy. Many a day my wife and I work for long hours after our regular jobs. Then, we work early the next morning before the kids are up, until it is time to go to our day jobs. My brother, my wife, and I often spend full weekends painting until our arms are so tired that we can barely hold a brush. On the positive side, we definitely eat and sleep well.

Our motto is, "We work like dogs, we eat like hogs, and we sleep like logs."

Pièce de résistance - Add feelings

What is your favorite memory?

It's probably something that happened to you that gives you a warm feeling whenever you think about it. If you can convert your favorite memory into a story, then you have a story that will move other people, and give them something that they will remember for a long time.

My favorite memory occurred when I was around four or five years old. My dad would come home from work and he would take my brother and me, with our baseball gloves, to the back yard. We would play catch for a while, then my dad would be the catcher, and my brother and I would take turns being the pitcher. My Dad would call out the strikes ("steeerike!") sometimes whip his glove off after a pitch and blow on his hand, pretending that the pitch was so fast that it hurt his hand.

I never wanted our games of catch to end. It still gives me a tingly feeling when I recall those afternoons with my dad. This is an example of the pure essence of being a dad.

There are other stories I think of as a "favorite memory: meeting my future wife for the first time; the birth of my son; going to a movie with my mom; or when I hit home run in my first baseball game. They are all attached to strong feelings. All make great stories.

To help jog your memory and to see how other people respond to the "favorite memory" question, check out this inspirational YouTube video *Fifty People, One Question – CHICAGO* at: http://bit.ly/1rDRLGk.

Lincoln's Lessons

1) Use stories as a teaching tool.

2) Motivate yourself to tell stories by viewing it as a way to reach your goals.

3) Not all stories have to be great. Even simple, bare bones stories can accomplish their purpose.

4) Tell stories that make you feel something inside.

8

How to "Lincolnize" Borrowed Stories

I do generally remember a good story when I hear it, but I never did invent anything original; I am only a retail dealer.

-- Abraham Lincoln

"Lincolnize" old stories

Most of Lincoln's stories were "borrowed" from other storytellers. Mr. Lincoln never claimed his stories were original. He modestly maintained,

> I don't make the stories mine by telling them.

Henry C. Whitney recalled that a judge once loaned Lincoln a joke book (the extremely popular *Joe Miller's Complete Jest Book*). Soon Lincoln had internalized the stories and was re-telling them, but with his own modifications and embellishments. Whitney said the stories were "Lincolnized."

Former Arizona Congressman and Lincoln acolyte, Mo Udall, said,

> A good joke (or story) is timeless, and most political jokes are recycled. You could take Abe Lincoln's joke book, substitute autos or airplanes for horses and carriages, change time and place, and end up with a witty, timely joke.

Finding and preserving stories

Stories can be found everywhere – books television, movies, church. Some of the best stories are the ones we hear from friends throughout the course of our day. The stories are out there like apples on a tree, ready to be picked. The key is to remember them.

In my case, when I hear a story that I want to remember, I immediately write it down. If I'm in my house, I write it in a notebook or in my desk calendar. I also carry recycled envelopes in my pocket to jot down story ideas, when I'm outside the house. They are especially useful when I am taking the dog for a walk, or going to church. When I return home, I transfer the story to my notebook or calendar.

The next step is to "Lincolnize" the story, or transform the story so that it is no longer just "a story" but it becomes "your" story.

The Lincoln storytelling template

Use this template to frame your story in the same electric style that Lincoln used to tell his stories. Follow Lincoln to reap the harvest of a typical Lincoln story and:

1. Connect with your listener.
2. Generate laughter.
3. Enlighten your listener.

Step One - Opening sentence

Segue from topic being discussed to the story:

"That reminds me of a when I . . ." or,

"Let me illustrate that point . . ." or,

"Speaking of . . . one time I when I was . . . ."

Personalize the story. Never start a story by saying "A man walked into a bar." Instead say, "I walked into a bar," or, "My friend, Frank, walked into a bar." Just jump into the story without prefacing it with "Here's a funny story" or "I heard a story the other day."

Step Two – Tell your story with pizzazz

Tell a story to illustrate your point:

"When I tried to make telephone calls to the U.S. I had to wait a long time . . . ."

Become one with the story. Give each character a personality.

Step Three – Thought provoking conclusion

Wrap up with a moral or humorous twist:

"If you don't shake every hand, you can't talk to Aunt Fran."

Place this succinct message of the story into your final sentence.

Lincoln's Lessons

1) "Lincolnize" your story by modifying if to fit your style and objectives.

2) When you find a good story, write it down before it slips away.

3) Use the three step Lincoln storytelling template to frame your stories.

9

Seven Traits that Infused Lincoln's Stories with Sizzling Energy

The greatness of Napoleon, Caesar or Washington is only moonlight to the sun of Lincoln. He was bigger than his country--bigger than all the Presidents together. He will live as long as the world lives.

-- Leo Tolstoy, 1909

To understand the core of Lincoln the storyteller, we must dig beneath the surface and look for the bed rock. Deep down, Lincoln's essence was composed of exceptional traits that saturated his stories with depth and meaning. His concern for others, his sense of purpose, his empathy, his forbearance of criticism, and other characteristics, made his stories a disarming tool that allowed him to connect with the people of his generation. Lincoln also inspires people of future generations and in foreign countries, like *War and Peace* author, Leo Tolstoy.

Seven key characteristics carried Lincoln to greatness both in storytelling and in life.

1) Communication skills (that Dale Carnegie would envy)

Gideon Welles, U.S. Secretary of the Navy, wrote that Lincoln was an effective communicator because he was "earnest, strong, honest, simple in style, and clear as crystal in his logic."

Of the four candidates running for the Republican nomination for the Presidency in 1860, Lincoln had the very least amount of experience. Compared to the other candidates, who were all political "heavy weights," Lincoln was considered a political "light weight."

It's like the scene in the movie *Rocky*, where a TV interview shows Rocky pounding frozen cow carcasses like punching bags in preparation for the big fight. The champion's trainer is watching the TV and says,

Hey, champ, you should see this guy that you're going to fight. It looks like he means business.

The champ is on the phone busily lining up endorsements for the fight and absentmindedly replies,

Yeah, I mean business too.

But you could see in his demeanor that he didn't really comprehend the approaching "tsunami-zilla" that Rocky represented, just as Lincoln's opponents underestimated him.

On the surface, Lincoln's rivals for the nomination had nothing to fear from him. Lincoln's only political experience on the national level consisted of two failed senate races and a single term in Congress, which he had served twelve years earlier. Contrary to Lincoln, the other three candidates for the nomination were widely known and respected by most Americans.

William Henry Seward, the front runner for the nomination, had been a celebrated U.S. senator from New York for more than a decade and governor of his state for two terms before he went to Washington, D.C.

Ohio's Salmon Chase, a lookalike of the monster (Peter Boyle) in *Young Frankenstein*, also had been both senator and governor, and had played a central role in the formation of the national Republican Party.

Edward Bates was a widely respected elder statesman, a delegate to the convention that had framed the Missouri Compromise, and a former congressman whose opinions on national matters were still widely sought.

Yet somehow, Lincoln, a political unknown, surprised almost everyone, and through some form of political *jujitsu*, outmaneuvered his opponents and captured the nomination.

In retrospect, we can see an explanation of how Lincoln accomplished this astounding feat.

Lincoln had a huge advantage in the crucial area of

communication and storytelling. Lincoln had an easy-going personality and a style of not directly attacking the opinions of others. Rather, he used persuasion and stories to win them over, resulting in no delegates at the convention being strongly opposed to him. When the other candidates split the vote, the affable Lincoln was the runaway "second choice" of the nominating convention. Lincoln could have been the poster boy for Dale Carnegie's book *How to Win Friends and Influence People.*

At the end of the day, Lincoln's victory was an extraordinary example of the power of storytelling. Lincoln's proficiency in storytelling eclipsed the experience and credentials of the other candidates.

2) Mastery of metaphors

Aristotle said,

To be a master of metaphor is a sign of genius, since a good metaphor implies intuitive perception of the similarity in dissimilars.

A recent study entitled *Presidential Leadership and Charisma: The Effects of Metaphor* concluded that,

Charismatic presidents used nearly twice as many metaphors than non-charismatic presidents.

Metaphors have naturally become a weapon wielded by all great political figures. Lincoln, a great fan of writings packed with rhetorical metaphors, for example *The Bible* and the works of Shakespeare, exercised that power as well as any other president.

Three of Lincoln's most notable metaphors were:

a) "A house divided against itself cannot stand," said by Lincoln during the Lincoln-Douglas debates in 1858, when Lincoln said (Lincoln and Stephen Douglas, "the Little Giant," were political opponents, Douglas being the more prominent from his long service in the U.S. Senate. Douglas once courted Mary Todd, who later became Mrs. Lincoln);

b) "It's best not to swap horses when crossing streams," which was Lincoln's campaign slogan for re-election as President in 1864.

c) Lincoln used this "snake-in-the-bed" analogy to explain his views on the complicated issue of slavery:

> If I saw a venomous snake crawling in the road, any would say I might seize the nearest stick and kill it. But if there was a bed newly made up, to which the children were to be taken, and it was proposed to take a batch of young snakes and put them there with them, I take it no man would say there was any question how I ought to decide! The New Territories are the newly made bed to which our children are to go, and it lies with the nation to say whether they shall have snakes mixed up with them or not.

Lincoln was saying that slavery should not expand to *The New Territories* acquired from the war with Mexico. With this metaphor the point could be easily grasped and shared with others. It had the legs of a viral internet video.

William Henry Seward, the favorite for the Republican nomination, tried to make the same point about slavery, but his metaphor was less effective. He said that allowing slavery in Kansas through the *Kansas-Nebraska Act* was like introducing a Trojan horse into the new territory. I can imagine Seward trying to fire up a puzzled audience by saying, in a deep, scary voice, "one dark and stormy night they would roll this giant wooden Trojan horse across the state line, and it was packed like sardines with pro-slavery supporters!"

I'm thinking, "Why cram people into a wooden horse when they could just walk across the border?" The unvarnished truth was that Seward's Trojan horse example did not have the same appeal to common people as did Lincoln's snake-in-the-bed story.

3) Indomitable sense of purpose

Lincoln said,

I am not bound to win, but I am bound to be true. I am not bound to succeed, but I am bound to live by the light that I have.

Early on in his career, Lincoln had a strong belief that he had a purpose to fulfill. He stated that he had a desire to "engrave" his name in history:

Every man is said to have his peculiar ambition, I have no other so great as that of being truly esteemed by fellow men, by rendering myself worthy of their esteem.

When the debate over slavery divided the country, Lincoln found his purpose was to preserve the Founding Fathers' ideal that "government of the people, by the people, for the people, shall not perish from the earth."

While Lincoln had a soft side, he also could be unbending when it came defending principles of liberty and justice. Here is how Frederick Douglass described Lincoln's approach to allowing the former slaves the right to vote:

> Having learned statesmanship while splitting rails, he always used the edge of the wedge first – and the fact that he used this at all meant that he would if need be, use the thick as well as the thin. He saw the absurdity of asking men to fight for a government which should degrade them and the meanness of enfranchising enemies and disfranchising friends.

In describing how he viewed his own leadership style Lincoln said,

> I walk slow but I never walk back.

4) Great empathy

Lincoln's stepmother, Sarah Bush Lincoln, described his kindness and empathy in this manner,

> Abe never gave me a cross word or look and never refused in fact, or even in appearance, to do anything I requested him. I never gave him a cross word in all my life. He was kind to everybody and to everything and always accommodated others if he could.

As President, Lincoln was often characterized as "compassionate" "kindhearted" and "generous" by the people who knew him best. Speaker of the House, Schuyler Colfax, once remarked,

> No man clothed with such vast power ever wielded it more tenderly and forbearingly.

Helen Nicolay, daughter of the President's private secretary said,

> Lincoln's crowning gift of political diagnosis was due to his sympathy, which gave him the power to forecast with uncanny accuracy what his opponents were likely to do.

Rather than criticize Southerners who supported slavery, Lincoln put himself in their place to experience their feelings and to understand their motives and desires. He never called *The Confederacy* or Jefferson Davis the enemy. In referring to the states that were dependent on slaves to work their estates, Lincoln observed,

> If slavery did not now exist amongst them, they would not introduce it. If it did now exist amongst us, we should not instantly give it up.

5) Embracing rivals

Author Doris Goodwin observed,

> Lincoln had the rare wisdom of temperament that consistently displayed generosity toward those that opposed him.

Lincoln held no grudges and nobly reached out to

maintain rapport with the men who defeated him in early political races. Lincoln put the goal of saving the government above his own ego and created a "team of rivals" by naming to his Cabinet the men he defeated for the Republican Presidential nomination. The thorny relationship between Edwin Stanton and Lincoln illustrates how far Lincoln would go to overlook personal offenses.

Stanton and Lincoln – Friendly enemies

An important patent case was to be tried in Chicago, and Philadelphia patent specialist George Harding hired Lincoln to serve as the lawyer for the case. Lincoln received an initial sum of money from Harding, and he began to prepare legal arguments for the case.

Later, the case was transferred to Cincinnati and Lincoln was replaced by the fastidious Edwin Stanton, a lawyer wound up tighter than Kloe Kardashian's corset at an all-you-can-eat pancake breakfast. However, Lincoln never received the memo of the change. For months, Lincoln continued working on the case. In late September, he set out for Cincinnati with his legal brief in hand. Kearns describes his encounter with Stanton and Harding:

> Arriving at the Burnet House where all the lawyers were lodged, he encountered Harding and Stanton as they left for the court. Lincoln introduced himself and proposed, "Let's go up in a gang."

> At this point, Stanton drew Harding aside and whispered, "Why did you bring that d---d long armed Ape here. He does not know anything and can do you no good."

The snubs continued throughout Lincoln's uncomfortable stay in Cincinnati. Lincoln took the humiliating offenses personally. Upon leaving Ohio, he wrote a friend:

> In reply to your request for me to come again I must say to you I never expect to be in Cincinnati again. I have nothing against the city, but things have so happened here as to make it undesirable for me ever to return here.

6) Putting personal offenses in context

The next time Lincoln and Stanton met, six years later, Lincoln was President. Instead of holding Stanton's egregious offense against him, Lincoln offered Stanton the post of Secretary of War. Lincoln recognized both Stanton's faults and talents. Like *Doctor Doom*, Stanton was an egotistical genius, but had the ability to complete complex tasks even under pressure-cooker circumstances.

Lincoln knew that people respond differently under pressure than they might under normal circumstances, and he did not let one action by a person define who that person was. In this case, Stanton had been shaken by the tragic deaths of his wife, daughter, and brother prior to replacing Lincoln as attorney for the patent case.

7) Knowing the power of forgiveness

Still, a less forgiving man than Lincoln might never have considered Stanton for a post in his cabinet. Despite what appeared to be an unholy marriage between good and evil, Stanton and Lincoln proved to be an excellent team. In the end, it was Stanton who stood by Lincoln's death bed and uttered the words,

Now he belongs to the ages.

Lincoln's Lessons

1) Assume an easy going personality.

2) Never directly attack the opinions of others.

3) Use stories to persuade and win people over, and no one will oppose you.

4) Proficiency in storytelling outweighs experience and credentials.

5) Win or lose, live by the light that you have.

6) Reach out and maintain rapport with your rivals.

10

My Favorite Stories & Quips by Lincoln

Lincoln's stories are like Lincoln himself. The more we know of them the more we like them.

-- Colonel Alexander K. McClure,
Yarns and Stories by Abraham Lincoln:
America's Greatest Storyteller

Here's a selection of my favorite stories and quips by Lincoln.

1) A big hay crop

Lincoln had heard a farmer brag about his hay crop one year. "We stacked all we could outdoors, and then we put the rest of it in the barn."

2) Kentucky Horse Sale

Lincoln told of the Kentucky horse sale where a small boy, the son of a horse trader, mounted a horse to show off its fine points. A man whispered, "Look here, boy, hain't that horse got the splints?" The boy replied, "Mister, I don't know what the splints is, but if it's good for him, he has it; if it ain't good for him, he ain't got it."

3) How to succeed

Give me six hours to chop down a tree and I will spend the first four sharpening the axe.

4) The chestnut horse

During the Lincoln-Douglas debates, Douglas twisted Lincoln's antislavery position into more shapes than *Gumby*. Lincoln replied that Douglas was a silver-tongued liar who could string together words and convince any man or woman that *a horse chestnut is the same as a chestnut horse.*

5) Campaign speech

Lincoln was giving a campaign speech before a very unfriendly crowd. At the end, someone yelled out, "I wouldn't vote for you if you were St. Peter himself!"

"My friend," replied Lincoln, "if I were St. Peter, you could not possible vote for me. You would not be in my district!"

6) Dog and pitchfork

While defending a man against an assault charge, Lincoln claimed it was more like self-defense, as in the case of a man he knew who was walking down the road with a pitchfork and was attacked by a very fierce dog. In trying to ward off the dog's attacks he stuck the prongs of the pitchfork into the animal and killed him. According to Lincoln, the dialogue that followed went like this:

"What made you kill my dog?" said the farmer.

"What made your dog try to bite me?" the man answered.

"But why didn't you go after him with the other end of your pitchfork?"

"Why didn't he come after me with his other end?"

At this point, Mr. Lincoln whirled about, in his long arms an imaginary dog, and pushed his tail toward the jury. The jury found Lincoln's client innocent.

7) No vices, no virtues

Riding at one time in a stage with an old Kentuckian who was returning from Missouri, Lincoln elicited the old gentleman's surprise by refusing to accept neither an offer of tobacco or French brandy.

When they separated that afternoon - the Kentuckian to take another stage bound for Louisville - he shook hands warmly with Lincoln, and said, good-humoredly:

"See here, stranger, you're a clever but strange companion. I may never see you again, and I don't want to offend you, but I want to say this: My experience has taught me that a man who has no vices has d——d few virtues. Good-day."

8) Little pigs

Lincoln read a rough draft of the *Emancipation Proclamation* to his Cabinet. They responded initially with a few comments, but soon everyone was putting his two-cents worth in with suggested changes.

"Gentlemen," said Lincoln, "this reminds me of the story of the man who had been away from home, and when he was coming back he was met by one of his farmhands, who greeted him after this fashion: 'Sir the little pigs are dead; and the sow's dead, too, but I didn't like to tell you all at once.' "

9) Don't trust generals or fish scales

Commenting to an old friend about one of his generals, Mr. Lincoln said, "He (the general) tells me that twelve thousand of Lee's soldiers have just been captured," Lincoln said. "But that doesn't mean anything; he's the biggest liar in Washington. You can't believe a word he says."

"He reminds me of an old fisherman I used to know who got such a reputation for stretching the truth that he bought a pair of scales and insisted on weighing every fish in the presence of witnesses."

"One day a baby was born next door, and the doctor borrowed the fisherman's scales to weigh the baby."

"It weighed forty-seven pounds."

10) Why shout hello!

A man was driving about the country in an open buggy, caught at night by a pouring rain. Passing a farmhouse, a man, apparently struggling with the effects of whisky, thrust his head out of the window and shouted loudly:

"Hello!"

The traveler stopped, despite his hurry for shelter, and asked what was wanted.

"Nothing of you!" was the blunt reply.

"Well, why are you shouting 'Hello' when people are passing?"

"Well, why are you passing by when people are shouting 'Hello'?"

11) Too many dogs

A group of politicians called on Lincoln, to implore the President to appoint some of their friends to a certain department. By way of refusal, the President told the following story:

"Gentlemen, the conditions in that department put me in mind of the time that a young friend and myself tried to court the daughters of a peppery widow living near our homes. The old lady kept a lot of hounds.

We had not been in the house long before one of the hounds came into the room, and lay down by the fire. In a little while another one came to the door. He didn't get in, for the old lady gave him a kick, saying: 'Get out of here! There are too many dogs in here now!'

We concluded to court other girls."

12) Keep floating

One stormy night a ship was wrecked off the coast of New Jersey and only one man survived the ordeal. The survivor grabbed a floating mast and was washed toward shore. Some kindhearted railroad workers tossed him a rope and pulled him toward the beach.

"You're saved!" they shouted. "Just show your ticket to the conductor."

With the waves still crashing around him, the drowning stranger resisted the efforts to pull him ashore.

"Stop!" he cried in a faint voice. "Tell me where I am! What country is this?"

They answered, "New Jersey."

The words had barely left their mouths when the soggy stranger let go of the rope and said, "I guess I'll float a little farther."

13) Lick any man in the crowd

When the enemies of General Grant were complaining to the President with emphatic and repeated demands that the Grant be removed from command, Mr. Lincoln remained firm. He would not consent to lose the services of so valuable a soldier. "Grant fights," said Lincoln in response to the charges made that Grant was a butcher, a drunkard, an incompetent, and a general who did not know his business.

"That reminds me of a story," President Lincoln said one day to an "anti-Grant" delegation.

"Out in my State of Illinois there was a man nominated for sheriff of the county. He was a good man for the office, brave, determined and honest, but not much of an orator. In fact, he couldn't talk at all. He couldn't make a speech to save his life.

His friends knew he was a man who would preserve the peace of the county and perform the duties devolving upon him all right, but the people of the county didn't know it. They wanted him to come out boldly on the platform at political meetings and state his convictions and principles. They had been used to speeches from candidates, and were somewhat suspicious of a man who was afraid to open his mouth.

At last the candidate consented to make a speech, and his friends were delighted. The candidate was on hand, and, when he was called upon, advanced to the front and faced the crowd. There was a glitter in his eye that wasn't pleasing, and the way he walked out to the front of the stand showed that he knew just what he wanted to say.

'Feller Citizens,' was his beginning, the words spoken quietly, 'I'm not a speakin' man; I ain't no orator, an' I never stood up before a lot of people in my life before.

I'm not goin' to make no speech, 'xcept to say that I can lick any man in the crowd!' "

11

My Favorite Stories about Lincoln

Mr. Lincoln's humor was a sparkling spring, gushing out of a rock – the gushing water had a somber background which made it all the brighter.

– David R. Locke
(pen name: Petroleum V. Nasby),
Lincoln's favorite humorist

1) Lincoln's kindness toward children

As a boy, William B. Thompson lived near Lincoln, then an attorney at law, in Springfield. Thompson recalled:

> Mr. Lincoln walked along with his hands behind him, gazing upward and noticing nobody. But it was usual for all of the boys in the neighborhood to speak to him as we met him. He had endeared himself to all of us by reason of the interest he took in us.
>
> When one of us spoke to him as he was walking along in his absorbed manner he would stop and acknowledge the greeting pleasantly. If the boy was small Mr. Lincoln would often take him up in his arms and talk to him. If the boy was larger Mr. Lincoln would shake hands and talk with him.
>
> If he didn't recall the face, he would ask the name, and if recognized it he would say, "Oh, yes; I remember you." If the boy was a comparative stranger Mr. Lincoln would treat him so pleasantly that the boy always wanted to speak to Mr. Lincoln after that whenever he met him.

2) Pluck a thistle

> Joshua F. Speed recalled watching with admiration as President Lincoln interacted with visitors a few weeks before he was assassinated.
>
> "Speed, die when I may," Lincoln told his longtime friend, "I want it said of me by those who know me best

to say that I always plucked a thistle and planted a flower where I thought a flower would grow."

3) Don't shoot too high

Lincoln's advice to lawyers, as noted by Herndon:

"Don't shoot too high. Aim lower, and the common people will understand you. They are the ones you want to reach—at least they are the ones you ought to reach. The educated and refined people will understand you, anyway. If you aim too high, your ideas will go over the heads of the masses and only hit those who need no hitting."

4) Lincoln swapping stories with Van Buren

In June, 1842, ex-President Martin Van Buren was journeying through Illinois, with a company of friends. When near Springfield they were delayed by bad roads, and were compelled to spend the night at an isolated rural inn. The accommodations at this place were very poor, and a few of the ex-President's Springfield friends proposed to go out to meet him and try to aid in entertaining him. Knowing Lincoln's ability as a story-teller, they begged him to go with them and aid in making their guest at the country inn pass the evening as pleasantly as possible.

Lincoln, with his usual good nature, went with them, and entertained the party for hours with graphic descriptions of Western life, anecdotes and witty stories.

There was a constant stream of brilliant anecdotes and funny stories, accompanied by loud laughter in which Van Buren bore his full share. Van Buren shared incidents and anecdotes of leading members of the New York bar, and going back to the days of Hamilton and Burr.

Van Buren later said his only complaint was,

His sides were sore for a week thereafter from laughing at Lincoln's stories.

5) Lightning rod

When Lincoln was a candidate for re-election to the Illinois Legislature in 1836, a meeting was held in the court house in Springfield, at which candidates of opposing parties were to speak.

George Forquer was a prominent citizen of Springfield. He had been a Whig, but became a Democrat – possibly to secure the position of Government Land Register from President Andrew Jackson. He had the largest and finest house in the city, and there was a striking addition to it, called a lightning-rod!

Forquer, although not a candidate, asked to be heard for the Democrats, to reply to Lincoln. He was a good speaker, and well known throughout the county. His special task that day was to attack and ridicule the young man from Salem.

Turning to Lincoln, who stood within a few feet of him, he said: "This young man must be taken down, and I am truly sorry that the task devolves upon me." He then proceeded to attack Lincoln in a very overbearing way, and with an air of great superiority. He was fluent and adept at rough sarcasm. He ridiculed Lincoln's appearance, dress, and opinions so fiercely that Lincoln's friends feared the he would be too embarrassed to respond.

Lincoln stood calm, but his flashing eye and pale cheek indicated his indignation. Lincoln took the podium and stated,

"The gentleman commenced his speech by saying that 'this young man,' alluding to me, must be taken down. I am not so young in years as I am in the tricks and the trades of a politician, but, live long or die young, I would rather die now than, like the gentleman (pointing to Forquer), change my politics and with the change receive an office worth $3,000 a year. And then, feel obliged to erect a lightning-rod over my house, to protect a guilty conscience from an offended God!"

6) Lincoln's dialect

On Jan. 28, 1862, George Templeton Strong, a New York lawyer, and Henry Ward Bellows, a Unitarian minister, called on the President. Strong, recorded the meeting in his diary and included Lincoln's dialect and exact phrasing.

In discussing the pressure from abolitionists for the President to take action against slavery, Lincoln said,

Wa-al that reminds me of a party of Methodist parsons that was traveling in Illinois when I was a boy, and had a branch to cross that was pretty bad — ugly to cross, ye know, because the waters was up. And they got considerin' and discussin' how they should git across it, and they talked about it for two hours, and one of 'em thought they had ought to cross one way when they got there, and another way, and they got quarrellin' about it, till at last an old brother put in, and he says, says he, "Brethren, this here talk ain't no use. I never cross a river until I come to it."

7) What Lincoln looked like when telling a story

Indiana Congressman, George W. Julian, recalled,

President Lincoln entered into the enjoyment of his stories with all his heart, and completely lived over again the delight he had experienced in telling them on previous occasions. When he told a particularly good story, and the time came to laugh, he would sometimes throw his left foot across his right knee, and clenching his foot with both hands and bending forward, his whole frame seemed to be convulsed with the effort to give expression to his sensations."

8) And tell it he would

Herndon describes an example of Lincoln's storytelling propensity:

On a winter morning, Mr. Lincoln might be seen

stalking towards, the market-house, basket in arm, his old gray shawl wrapped around his neck, his little boy Willie or Tad running along at his heels asking a thousand boyish questions, while his father, in deep abstraction, neither heeded, nor heard.

If a friend met or passed him, and he awoke from his reverie, something would remind him of a story he had heard in Indiana, and tell it he would, and there was no alternative but to listen.

9) The end in view

Ward Hill Lamon (Lincoln's law partner, 1852-57, and later bodyguard for the President) wrote,

> Mr. Lincoln was from the beginning of his circuit-riding the light and life of the court. The most trivial circumstance furnished a back-ground for his wit. The following incident, which illustrates his love of a joke, occurred in the early days of our acquaintance.

> I, being at the time on the infant side of twenty-one, took particularly pleasure in athletic sports. One day when we were attending the circuit court which met at Bloomington. I was wrestling near the court house with someone who had challenged me to a trial, and in the scuffle made a large rent [tear] in the rear of my trousers.

> Before I had time to make any change, I was called into court to take up a case. The evidence was finished. I, being the Prosecuting Attorney at the time, got up to

address the jury. Having on a somewhat short coat, my misfortune was rather apparent.

One of the lawyers, for a joke, started a subscription paper which was passed from one member of the bar to another as they sat by a long table fronting the bench, to buy a pair of pantaloons for Lamon – "he being," the paper said, "a poor but worthy young man." Several put down their names with some ludicrous subscription, and finally the paper was laid by someone in front of Mr. Lincoln, he being engaged in writing at the time.

He quietly glanced over the paper, and, immediately taking up his pen, wrote after his name, "I can contribute nothing to the end in view."

10) Lincoln trades horses

While riding the circuit, Lincoln got into a discussion about horse-trading, and the discussion ended with an agreement that Lincoln and Judge David Davis would trade horses at nine o'clock the following morning. Both horses were to be unseen until the moment of the trade. Promptly at nine Judge Davis appeared, leading the sorriest specimen of a horse ever seen in those parts. In a few moments Lincoln appeared, carrying a wooden sawhorse over his shoulder. He set down the sawhorse and inspected the judge's animal.

"Well judge," he said, "that's the first time I ever got the worst of it in a horse trade."

11) General Cass' eating habits

When Lincoln was a representative in Congress (1847-1849), General Lewis Cass was a candidate for the Presidency, and his Democratic supporters were trying to pad his resume comparing him to the popular former president, Andrew Jackson. Lincoln used public records to take Cass down a notch by pointing out his abuse of government benefits. Lincoln found that Cass had collected benefits simultaneously as both Governor of the Michigan Territory and as Superintendent of Indian Affairs.

Lincoln said, "The records show that he (Cass) not only did the labor of several, but that he often did it at several places, many hundreds of miles apart, at the same time. And, at eating too, his capacities are shown to be quite wonderful."

At one point, Cass ate ten rations a day in Michigan, ten in Washington, and five a day on the road between them.

Lincoln concluded, "By all means, make him President, gentlemen. He will feed you bounteously, if there is any left after he shall have helped himself."

12) Shirt on backwards

Once, when Lincoln was pleading a case, the opposing lawyer had all the advantage of the law. The weather was warm, and his opponent, as was admissible in frontier courts, pulled off his coat and vest as he grew warm in the argument.

At that time, shirts with buttons behind were not unusual, and the other attorney was wearing just such a shirt. Lincoln took in the situation at once. Lincoln understood the prejudices of the local people against pretension, or affectation of superior social rank.

He stood and said: "Gentlemen of the jury, having justice on my side, I don't think you will be at all influenced by the gentleman's pretended knowledge of the law, when you see he does not even know which side of his shirt should be in front."

There was a general laugh, and Lincoln's case was won.

13) Putting on airs

Lincoln used the telegraph as his primary means of communication with his armies in the field, and to put starch in the spines of his timid generals.

Lincoln had a particular general who liked to send dispatches that were always headed: "Headquarters in the Saddle." Every day, or every other day, Lincoln would get one of these messages entitled "Headquarters in the Saddle." He got quite annoyed with this, but he kept quiet, as he normally did, until, finally, one day somebody asked him about this general and about this habit of heading all these dispatches "Headquarters in the Saddle."

Lincoln said, "It seems to me that the general has his

headquarters where his hindquarters ought to be."

14) Lincoln saves a bird

Lincoln was travelling with a group of lawyers and the group happened to ride past a little bird which had fallen from the nest and lay fluttering on the ground. It was noticed by several of the horsemen, including Mr. Lincoln.

After riding a short distance he said to his companions, "Wait a moment, I want to go back," and as they stopped for him he was seen to ride back, dismount, and pick up the little fledgling and carefully put it in the nest.

When he rejoined the party they said: "Why, Lincoln, you need not have stopped for such a trifle as that." Pausing a little while, he answered, quietly, "Well, I feel better for doing it, anyhow."

15) Story-telling contest

Lew Wallace (lawyer, Union General, and author of *Ben Hur*) described Lincoln at a joke telling contest between lawyers.

Lincoln arrested my attention early, partly by his stories, partly by his appearance. His hair was thick, coarse, and defiant; it stood out in every direction. His features were massive, nose long, eyebrows protrusive, mouth large, cheeks hollow, eyes gray and always responsive to the humor. He smiled all the time, but never once did he laugh outright.

His hands were large, his arms slender and disproportionately long. His legs were a wonder, particularly when he was in narration; he kept crossing and uncrossing them; sometime it actually seemed he was trying to tie them into a bow-knot. His dress was more than plain; no part of it fit him. Altogether I thought him the gauntest, quaintest, and most positively ugly man. Still, when he was speaking, my eyes did not quit his face. He held me in unconsciousness.

16) Lincoln meets Frederick Douglass

Fredrick Douglass, African-American social reformer, orator, and anti-slavery leader, said of Lincoln,

From the first moment of my interview with him I seemed to myself to have been acquainted with him for years. For while he was among the most solid men I ever met he was among the most transparent.

17) Playing marbles

One evening, an extremely busy and weary Lincoln was called to the reception room to see Attorney General James Speed. He had called to introduce a friend and, seeing the weary look on the President's face, began to apologize.

"I am very sorry, Mr. President," said Mr. Speed, "to disturb you."

"Speed," he replied, "you remind me of a story of Henry Ward Beecher. One Sunday as he was going to preach, he saw some boys playing marbles in the street. He stopped and looked at them very hard. 'Boys,' he said, 'I am scared at what I see.' "

"Then," replied one of the boys, "why don't you run away?"

18) Coaching "Pipes"

F. B. Carpenter, who spent several months in the White House painting Lincoln's portrait, recalled a half-hour's entertainment given there by Stephen Massett, better known as "Jeems Pipes of Pipesville." Carpenter observed,

> His repertoire included a series of comic imitations, one of which, a take-off on a stammering man, was especially amusing to the President. After the "lecture" Lincoln, in congratulating 'Pipes,' ventured a suggestion. "I once knew a man who invariably whistled with his stammering," he said - and gave an imitation. "Now if you could get in a touch of nature like that it would be irresistibly ludicrous." Pipes approved the idea, rehearsed the whistle until he had mastered it to Lincoln's satisfaction, and used it in subsequent performances.

19) Lincoln's gentle reprimand

Lincoln gave this official reprimand to a young officer who had been court-martialed for a quarrel with one of his associates. The reprimand is probably the gentlest on record.

> Quarrel not at all. No man resolved to make the most of himself can spare time for personal contention. Still less can he afford to take all the consequences, including the vitiating of his temper and the loss of self-control. Yield larger things to which you can show no more than equal right; and yield lesser ones, though clearly your own.

> Better give your path to a dog than be bitten by him in contesting for the right. Even killing the dog would not cure the bite.

20) Let the elephant run

Charles A. Dana, Assistant Secretary of War, received information that a high ranking Southern official named Thompson was about to escape to Liverpool.

Calling upon Edwin Stanton (Secretary of War), Dana was referred to Mr. Lincoln. Dana describes his meeting with the President,

> The President was at the White House, business hours were over, Lincoln was washing his hands. "Hallo, Dana," said he, as I opened the door, "what is it now?"

> "Well, sir I said, "here is the Provost Marshal of Portland, who reports that Jacob Thompson is to be in town tonight, and inquires what orders we have to give."

"What does Stanton say?" he asked.

"Arrest him," I replied.

Well," he continued, drawling his words, "I rather guess not. When you have an elephant on your hands, and he wants to run away, better let him run."

Historical note: This incident took place on Lincoln's last day on earth. Lincoln was destined to go to Ford's Theater that night, April 14, 1865, to watch the play "Our American Cousin."

12

Get Out There and Touch Hearts, Minds, and Funny Bones

Always bear in mind that your own resolution to succeed is more important than any one thing.

– Abraham Lincoln

Abraham Lincoln may no longer walk this Earth, but his message continues to beckon us.

Through the example of his life, Abraham Lincoln shares a truth with us that, like the Rock of Gibraltar, is immovable and unalterable. He is entrusting us with his version of the *Philosopher's Stone,* but instead of converting any metal to gold, it has the power to transform strangers into friends. Lincoln proved the value of stories in his liberal use of them to achieve his extravagantly lofty goals. If we follow the path blazed by Lincoln, we too can navigate through life, our stories preceding us, obstacles dropping like chain-sawed trees before us.

In our persistently fast paced and burdensome lives, it's easy to feel a little discombobulated. We can reorient our inner compass needle to true north by relying on stories to see us through. You may not share Lincoln's burning desire to be President, but whatever your goals may be, stories are sure tools in achieving them.

Prepare yourself to tell stories

If you haven't already started, you can begin now:

1. Compile a "storytelling" notebook

2. Memorize and practice stories

3. Adapt and personalize your stories

4. Add a moral, or a humorous ending, to your stories

5. Use self-deprecating humor

I encourage you to practice telling stories to everyone you meet. Think of it as Lincoln channeling his storytelling through you. To take the pressure off, sometimes I tell myself, "I'm only practicing telling stories. This doesn't really count."

Think of your spouse, children, co-workers, friends, relatives, and new acquaintances, as people who all could benefit from hearing a story. Yet, they may be blissfully oblivious of their need, and unaware of the impending good fortune they are about to receive.

A story at the doctor's office

While I was working on this book, I started to become aware of all the people who are a part of my life, but with whom I rarely interact. I now find that I have become bolder and more secure after carefully observing Lincoln's storytelling techniques. I'm much more inclined to reach out and share a story with someone.

For example, the other day, I accompanied my wife, Angy, to visit her doctor to have a pain in her hand checked out. I was in the room when the doctor examined her, and the doctor said he would print out his instructions on how to care for her sore hand. At that moment, one of the stories in my "Storytelling Notebook" popped into my mind and I shared it. It just rolled off my lips like a cash register receipt. I said,

You know, Doc, I'm glad you print out the instructions. It helps avoid confusion.

I took an 89 year-old friend of mine, Bill, in for a physical last week. A few days later I saw the Bill walking down the street with a gorgeous young lady on his arm.

I said, "Bill, what do you think you're doing?"

Bill raised his eyebrows and replied, "I'm just doing what the doctor said, 'Get a hot mamma and show her the town.' "

With an exasperated voice, I said, "That's not what the doctor said. He said you have a heart murmur and you should slow down."

Without written instructions, Bill just selectively hears whatever he wants to hear.

Note how I "Lincolnized" the story by making my real friend, Bill, the protagonist. In telling the story, I use an "old geezer" voice for Bill, a deep authoritative voice for me. I also tacked on a little moral at the end.

Angy rolled her eyes when she heard me begin to tell my story, but in truth, the story had the effect of breaking the ice in the doctor's formal style. The doctor responded to the story by laughing and subsequently treating me in a much friendlier manner. Instead of just looking at my wife when he spoke, now he established eye contact with me, too. Like Joshua's trumpets at Jericho, because of my story told to the doctor, the walls came tumbling down.

Today is the day

Stories were Lincoln's road to greatness and they can be ours too. To be successful, we don't need magic beans or Ninja tricks, we just need stories. Any occasion that we can imagine is an appropriate time to share a story with someone.

Lincoln said,

"I will prepare and someday my chance will come."

Today is your day. Your chance has arrived.

Lincoln's Lessons

1) Use stories to remove obstacles from your path.

2) Rely on storytelling to stay focused when the going gets rough.

3) "Channel" Lincoln stories through you to others.

4) To begin with, tell yourself that you are just practicing telling stories. Fruits will come regardless.

5) Use stories from your Storytelling Notebook to break the ice with someone.

6) Don't wait to tell stories until the magic beans arrive. They're not coming. Begin now.

Bibliography

Abraham Lincoln's Classroom.
http://www.abrahamlincolnsclassroom.org

Browne, Francis F. 1866. *The Every-Day Life of Abraham Lincoln*. N.D. Thompson Publishing Company.

De Regniers, Beatrice Schenk. 1965. *The Abraham Lincoln Joke Book*. Scholastic Inc.

DeRose, Chris. 2013. *Congressman Lincoln*. Threshold Editions.

Goodwin, Doris Kearns. 2006. *Team of Rivals: The Political Genius of Abraham Lincoln*. Simon and Schuster.

Herndon, William H. and Jesse William Weik. 1888. *Herndon's Lincoln: The True Story of a Great Life*. Obscure Press.

Hertz, Emmanuel. 1939. *Lincoln Talks: A biography in anecdote*. The Viking Press, Inc. http://archive.org/stream/lincolntalksbiog00hert/lincolntalksbiog00hert_djvu.txt.

Jennison, Keith W. 1965. *The Humorous Mr. Lincoln*. Bonanza Books.

Katz, Mark. 2004. *Clinton and Me: A Real Life Political Comedy*. Miramax.

Kunhardt III, Philip B., Peter W. Kunhardt, and Peter W. Kunhardt Jr. 2008. *Looking for Lincoln: The Making of an American Icon*. Alfred A. Knopf.

Lamon, Ward Hill. 1895. *Recollections of Abraham Lincoln 1847-1865*. University of Nebraska Press.

Masur, Louis P. 2012. "Lincoln Tells a Story." January 27, *New York Times*.

McClure, Alexander K. 1901. *Yarns and Stories by Abraham Lincoln: America's Greatest Storyteller*. E-Book. http://www.gutenberg.org/files/2517/2517-h/2517-h.htm

Miller, Joe and John Mottley. 1859. *Joe Miller's Complete Jest Book*. E-book. https://archive.org/details/joemillerscomple00mill. H.G. Bohn

Mr. Lincoln and Friends. http://www.mrlincolnandfriends.org/

Riggio, Ronald E., Shana Levin, Renford Reese. 2005. "Presidential Leadership and Charisma: The Effects of Metaphor." *The Leadership Quarterly,* Volume 16, Issue 2, April 2005, Pages 287–294.

Sandburg, Carl. 1982. *Abraham Lincoln: The Prairie Years and The War Years*. Harcourt Brace Javanovich.

Thomas, Benjamin J. 2002. *Lincoln's Humor and Other Essays*. University of Illinois Press.

Udall, Mo. 1987. *Too Funny to be President*. Henry Holt & Company.

Wheeler, Tom. 2006. *Mr. Lincoln's T-mails: The Untold Story of How Abraham Lincoln Used the Telegraph to Win the Civil War*. HarperCollins.

Whitney, Henry C. 1892. *Life on the Circuit with Lincoln*. E-book. Estes and Lauriet. *http://lcweb2.loc.gov//service/lawlib/law0001/2009/200 90012025344a/20090012025344a.pdf*

Wilson, Douglas L., and Rodney O. Davis. 1998. *Herndon's Informants: Letters, Interviews, and Statements about Abraham Lincoln*. University of Illinois Press.

Abraham Lincoln and Jefferson Davis

Appendix

Abraham Lincoln Timeline

1809   February 12, Abraham Lincoln born in Nolan Creek, Kentucky to Thomas Lincoln and Nancy Hanks.

1816   The Lincoln family moves to Pigeon Creek, Indiana. Young Abe observes his father's storytelling.

1818   Nancy Hanks Lincoln dies.

1819   Thomas Lincoln marries the widow, Sarah Bush Johnson. Young Abe relishes her collection of books, especially *Aesop's Fables*.

1830   The Lincolns move to Decatur, Illinois.

1831   Abe moves to New Salem to work as a clerk in a general store, telling stories to customers.

1832   Lincoln is a losing candidate for the Illinois General Assembly.

        Serves as a Captain during the Blackhawk War.

1834   Lincoln runs again for Illinois General Assembly. Changing strategy, he visits every house in the district and tells stories. Lincoln wins.

1836	Lincoln receives law license.
1837	Lincoln moves to Springfield and begins practicing law, using stories to sway juries.
1842	Marries Mary Todd.
1846	Elected to U.S. House of Representatives.
1855	Fails in quest to become U.S. Senator.
1858	Lincoln runs for U.S. Senate against Stephen A. Douglas, and loses election.
1860	Lincoln wins the Republican nomination for President over more qualified candidates by not directly attacking the opinions of others. Instead, he persuades with stories.
	Elected as 16th U.S. president.
	Southern states secede from the Union.
1864	Re-elected as President.
1865	April 9, General Lee surrenders to General Grant and the Civil War ends.
	April 15, Lincoln assassinated.

Index

About the Author

Terry Sprouse is a self-proclaimed Lincoln-holic. Since reading Carl Sandburg's "Abraham Lincoln," which fortuitously fell into his hands as a literature-starved Peace Corps Volunteer in Honduras in 1986, he has been captivated and inspired by this legendary figure. Terry now writes books and delivers speeches and seminars to groups about Mr. Lincoln's storytelling, & other topics. Terry and his wife, Angy, live in Tucson, Arizona with their two above average teenage boys.